I0374905

Original title:
Watering Can Dreams

Author: Oliver Bennett
ISBN HARDBACK: 978-1-80581-816-8
ISBN PAPERBACK: 978-1-80581-343-9
ISBN EBOOK: 978-1-80581-816-8

Liquid Light

In the garden, I laugh and play,
Chasing shadows that dance away.
With every splash, a giggle escapes,
My flowers bloom in comical shapes.

Leaves wear hats, a leafy parade,
As rabbits join in the escapade.
Mischief flows from the spout like a tune,
Beneath the quirky afternoon moon.

Bees buzz in disco, it's quite a sight,
Sipping nectar, they take flight.
I swear there's a worm with a top hat too,
In this wacky garden, all dreams are true.

Laughter echoes, the sun sets bright,
Endless giggles until the night.
With friendship and fun, we splash around,
In our own liquid light, joy is found.

Reflections in the Soil

In muddy puddles, I see my fate,
A crow with glasses declares it great.
My rubber boots squelch, a funny sound,
As worms throw parties beneath the ground.

Frogs in tuxedos serenade the flies,
While ants line dance beneath the skies.
Each raindrop's giggle a sweet little note,
And even the daisies begin to gloat.

Reflections shimmer, all out of place,
A snail dressed fancy, oh what a face!
With each drop that falls, the world gets bright,
In this muddy chaos, everything's right.

Bubbling laughter fills up the air,
Every little creature joins in the flair.
So come take a dip in this joyful soil,
Where the puddles sing, and happiness boils!

Journeys Through the Rain

Umbrellas spin like tops in the breeze,
Dancing wildly, as if they please.
My hat's taken off by a mischievous gust,
While raindrops perform their own wacky thrust.

Splashing puddles, a joyful crew,
Each leap reveals a squishy view.
In every storm, a giggle is found,
As rubber ducks float all around.

Clouds grumble softly, but I don’t care,
I twirl and spin, a carefree affair.
With every splash, my laughter ignites,
We're making memories, oh what delights!

So let it rain, let it pour with glee,
Adventure awaits, just look and see.
As we dance through this whimsical lane,
We’re on a journey, oh, through the rain!

Raindrop Reverberations

In the garden, a splash, a puddle,
A frog leaps high, oh what a muddle,
Worms dance like they're in a show,
While daisies giggle and flowers glow.

A bucket hat floats on a breeze,
The garden gnomes laugh with such ease,
A sprinkler spins, so wild and free,
Chasing ants like a game of spree.

The clouds above start to play peek,
A squirrel trips, oh what a cheek!
Raindrops drum on tin and leaves,
While mushrooms pop out like they're thieves.

Each droplet sings a funny tune,
As sunbeams sneak in, oh too soon,
A tango sprouts in muddy ballet,
In this patch, we dance the day away.

Nourishing the Seeds of Tomorrow

With each sprinkle, a tickle, a tease,
The beans stretch up with grace and ease,
They whisper secrets to the snails,
While lettuce dreams of ocean gales.

A sprinkle here, a splash right there,
Sunflowers sway with boisterous flair,
A rabbit hops, but trips on grass,
While daisies giggle as they pass.

The carrots push through, bold and bright,
They plot a plunge in the moonlight,
Radishes roll like a bowling game,
In veggie land, it’s never the same.

Each seedling chats with roots below,
As wind plays tricks on seeds in tow,
This garden’s magic lies in jest,
With nature's laughter at its best.

Gentle Currents of Inspiration

In the pond, fish paint with no brush,
Ripples giggle, they bring a hush,
Water lilies wear crown-like hats,
While frogs serenade tuxedoed bats.

A boat made of leaves drifts along,
With dragonflies singing a busy song,
Each splash is a giggle, so sweet,
As turtles tiptoe on their tiny feet.

The wise old heron, poised like a king,
Pauses to ponder the joy that spring brings,
With every wave, the laughter awakes,
As minnows play tag, and the grass quakes.

A wave nudges a duckling's rear,
The splashes are filled with giggles and cheer,
And as the sun melts into night,
The pond replays its splashing delight.

Embrace of the Earth's Tender Flow

Overflowing cups, a chaotic scene,
The gardener's trip, a clumsy routine,
With tumbles and stumbles, spills galore,
As flowers giggle asking for more.

A rainbow spills from the watering spout,
While bees buzz loudly, roundabout,
A butterfly, wings soaked with cheer,
Wonders how it all grew from here.

The sun chuckles under his hat,
As clouds play tag with a friendly spat,
Each drop of joy a silly prank,
In gardens where magic and colors rank.

Even weeds wear smiles in their own way,
Tall and proud, they join the fray,
In this silly dance of sprout and bloom,
Nature laughs and dispels all gloom.

Radiance in the Rain

Puddles shine like diamonds bright,
Dancing raindrops take their flight.
Umbrellas flip in gusty cheer,
I splash around without a fear.

Giggling grass beneath my shoes,
Worms are wearing their own snooze.
Clouds switch hats with playful grace,
Yet here I am, a soggy face.

Roots of the Heart

I dug a hole, and guess what grew?
A pair of socks that I once knew!
Confused, I thought they'd sprout some cheer,
But now they just smell of the pier.

With every spade, I took a chance,
Found my lost shoe, forgot to dance.
Roots twist and turn in a wobbly way,
My garden dreams sprout socks, hooray!

Silken Streams

Streams of silk run through my yard,
Chasing butterflies, oh how they bard!
Ribbons tumble, twirl, and play,
I think they're planning a fashion day.

Squirrels join in, dressed absurd,
In leafy hats, they're quite the herd.
Fashion shows in nature's glade,
With acorns cast as the grand parade!

A Garden’s Secret

Beneath the leaves, a secret lies,
With gnomes and fairies in disguise.
They heed the call of the morning sun,
And brew tea with sprinkles, just for fun.

Frisky rabbits take their sips,
While singing songs that flip and skip.
Whispers dance ‘round the sweetest blooms,
In my garden, laughter looms.

Drifting Dreams on Gentle Currents

A bucket on my head, I float,
Chasing clouds that look like a goat.
My dreams are sails on a little boat,
Hoping for rain, oh what a quote.

The fish wink at me as I glide,
Splashing water like it’s a slide.
I catch a tune from the river's tide,
Where jokes and giggles always abide.

Hallowed Grounds of Hope

In the garden, plants wear hats,
Sunflowers giggle, how they chat!
My tomato grows a funny spout,
Whispers wishes, and jokes about.

The daisies drink from cups of tea,
Telling stories of how they're free.
With every sip, they shout with glee,
In hallowed grounds, life's a spree!

A Symphony of Liquid Longings

In puddles, I play with my feet,
Each splash a note, oh what a treat!
Raindrops tap dance on the street,
A symphony that can’t be beat.

The hose sings songs of summer cheer,
As I prance, splashing far and near.
Buckets clatter, laugh without fear,
In this liquid world, fun is here!

Cascade of Colorful Intentions

Colors trickle down the spout,
A rainbow parade, what's this about?
With every splash, I twist and shout,
Intentions painted, there's no doubt.

The garden hose takes off to play,
Chasing butterflies, hip-hip-hurray!
Sprinkler spin, oh what a display,
In cascades of dreams, joy leads the way!

Pouring Hope

With a can in hand, I spill my cheer,
Watering weeds that never appear.
I swear I saw blooms, bright and so bold,
But they're just rocks, or so I'm told.

I dance with my hose like a mad old soul,
Convinced every droplet plays a role.
The flowers chuckle, they think it's a joke,
As I chat with the dirt and think it bespoke.

My garden's a circus, all wild and free,
Where carrots wear hats, just look and see!
I sprinkle my dreams on the random grass,
Hoping one day, I'll grow a brass.

Yet every sprout seems to take its time,
While I try to rhyme with the sound of the thyme.
A comedy show hosted right in my yard,
With punchlines of peas that are just too hard.

Raindrop Reveries

In my mind, there's a cloud on a permanent spree,
Dropping ideas like raindrops, oh whee!
Each splash that I hear sounds like laughter to me,
As daisies tell jokes, with an air of esprit.

The puddles are giggling, splashing away,
Where are the fish—did they swim out to play?
I send them invitations, but they're quite aloof,
Complaining they won't fit under my roof.

A rainbow appears, wearing goofy shades,
Telling puns to the drought as it parades.
"Water me please, I can't take the heat!"
While the sun just chuckles, ignoring the treat.

I dawdle and splash, what a hilarious sight,
Turning gloomy grey skies into giggly delight.
Who needs a fortune, when rain's on your side,
With humor distilled like a whimsical tide?

Seeds Beneath the Surface

Beneath all that dirt, seeds chatter and plot,
What grows in that darkness? They think it a lot.
A mushroom's a hat that a sprout longs to wear,
While dirt worms are gossiping without a care.

A seedling named Larry dreams big in his bed,
Imagining how he'll one day be fed.
"I'll stretch for the skies, and I'll twist with the breeze,
While telling all flowers to stop with the tease!"

They argue in whispers, decibels go down,
Saying who'll wear the biggest bloom crown.
A sunflower scoffs, "It's mine, can't you see?"
But deep down they know it's all just make-believe.

So they laugh and they wiggle, all snug underground,
As a comedy club of roots spins around.
Each thought in the soil is a humorous gem,
Waiting to sprout, like a quirky diadem.

Sprouts of Imagination

With a sprinkle of luck and a dash of fun,
I planted some dreams, oh wouldn't you run?
To see what would sprout in the sun's bright glow,
Like puppets in soil, with a comic show.

Tiny leaves wiggle, they twist and they shout,
"I'm busting with ideas, I'm turning about!"
They boast of their plans to reach for the sky,
While dodging the raindrops that thought they were sly.

"Oh, look at me!" cried a bold little bean,
"I'm sprouting my wings, you know what I mean?"
But the daisies just snicker, "Don't take it too far,
You'll end up more tangled than a nutty bazaar."

Yet everyone giggles, with roots intertwined,
Creating a ruckus that's one of a kind.
In the garden of dreams, where silliness reigns,
Each sprout a comedian, breaking all chains.

Atmosphere of Abundance

In a garden where gnomes dance,
Sunflowers wear hats, what a chance!
The puddles giggle with delight,
Chasing raindrops, oh, what a sight!

Sprinklers twirling like ballerinas,
Their water-choreography's so clean-a!
Bees buzz along to the tune,
As carrots wiggle beneath the moon.

A rock with a smile sits at the gate,
Telling jokes about food on a plate.
Each petal whispers, “Pick me, pick me!”
While squirrels debate if it’s time for tea.

With laughter and spritzers, joy we spread,
In our patch of green, worries shed.
Come frolic with us, don’t be shy,
In the realm where dreams can sprout and fly.

Quenching the Thirst

A berry in blue wears a tiny crown,
While thirsty ants in a line march down.
With tiny buckets, they seek a well,
To fill their cups and dance like hell!

The daisies shop for lemonade,
At the water fountain, their efforts displayed.
“Slice of citrus?” they giggle with cheer,
The gossip of petals floats far and near.

A frog on a lily sings with glee,
“Rain dance party! Come join me!”
Chasing droplets, they leap and bound,
Until the clouds turn into a sound.

The sun peeks out, with a wink and a grin,
As the garden’s laughter bubbles from within.
Every sip of joy is a splashing delight,
In a world where wonder is always in sight.

Harvesting Light

In a patch of sun, the veggies scheme,
Carrots plotting a daylight dream.
Tomatoes giggle, dressing up bright,
For a dance at dusk, what a sight!

The corn is a tall, proud, silly king,
Wearing a crown made of mashed potato bling.
Eggplants chatter, all sleek and fine,
While cucumbers form a conga line.

Even the weeds join the riotous fun,
"Who needs a scythe when we can run?"
The radishes show moves from the '90s,
With rhythms fresh and flows so shiny.

As hues of sunset paint us gold,
In this lot of laughs, hair's never old.
Gather the glow, let your heart take flight,
For in this garden, we harvest light.

The Infinite Garden

In a realm where squirrels wear sunglasses,
And dandelions throw showy jazzes.
The sun rolls out like a fuzzy rug,
While mushrooms dance with a roguish shrug.

Lettuce laughing with tales of the moon,
As tomatoes burst into a joyous tune.
A butterfly lands with a snicker and twirl,
Enlivening dreams in a leafy swirl.

Vines entwine, having a debate,
"Who's the tallest? I think it's fate!"
The carrots listen, shaking their tops,
While radishes play hopscotch with hops.

With each drop of rain, we all grin wide,
In this vast spread, we can't help but glide.
So come, my friend, let your worries melt,
In this infinite garden, pure joy is felt.

Flood of Aspiration

A spout with dreams inside, oh my!
Sprinkling wishes as they fly.
With every tip, a splash of cheer,
I plant my hopes; they sprout right here.

Each droplet dances, bold and bright,
Making mundane moments feel just right.
As I pour passion, the flowers grin,
Who knew that joy starts from within?

Beneath the sun, my visions grow,
Thirsty thoughts, they steal the show.
With humor perched upon my side,
My dreams are wild, they can't abide!

So here I stand, with laughter spry,
A garden full of glee, oh my!
I tip the spout, let the giggles flow,
In this charming patch, merriment grows!

Soaked in Possibility

With a pitcher fit for dreams so grand,
I braved the garden, shovel in hand.
Pouring puddles of sheer delight,
Mud on my shoes, oh what a sight!

My little plants, they chuckle and sway,
As I dance around, in a splashy ballet.
They beg for water, but I splash them more,
What fun it is to create a chore!

A hose, my friend, in this wacky game,
Twists and turns, it's never the same.
I whirl and twirl, in a water-lake quest,
Soaked in possibility, I feel the best!

With raindrops laughing, I join the spree,
Every sip, a drop of glee.
Beneath the sunny skies overhead,
In this wild garden, I won't be fed!

Streams of Serenity

In the stream that winds through this daydream,
Float silly thoughts like a wobbly beam.
With fish that giggle and waves that dance,
I bike on laughter; slip into a trance.

Splashes of joy from my copper can,
Who knew gardens could spin up a plan?
Chasing clouds and yellow beams of sun,
In my garden, simply having fun!

As rainbows form in a critter delight,
My garden's a circus, oh what a sight!
A parade of petals, a troupe of cheer,
Each drop a chuckle, each giggle sincere.

So I let the waters flow with glee,
A river of smiles just for me.
In this oasis where whimsy reigns,
Every sprout whispers, joy's true gains!

Heartbeats in a Patch

In a land where puns grow, I'm blissfully spent,
With heartbeat blooms, where laughter is meant.
My garden of jests is a curious sight,
With petals that giggle and roots that ignite.

I water with whimsy, not a care in the world,
Twirling with joy as my wishes unfurled.
Each droplet sparkles, a story to tell,
In this patch of laughter, life's simply swell!

With nectar of chuckles, I stroll and I trot,
Wishful blooms are all that I've got.
In the melody of nature, I'm serenely caught,
A patch of delight, life's truest thought!

So dance with your dreams, in this lively scene,
Where heartbeats rhythm, and laughter's routine.
In my patch of happiness, I'm loving the view,
With every sprinkle, joy's coming anew!

Blooming in the Abyss

In a garden of laughter, plants wear their hats,
Sunflowers giggle as they rock with the cats.
Dandelions dance with a hint of a twirl,
While radishes plot how to give peas a whirl.

A cactus, perplexed, tries to make a friend,
But every time it hugs, it's a prickly end.
Meanwhile, the roses stage a soap opera slice,
As bees buzz around with their gossip so nice.

Down by the pond, the lilies play chess,
A frog in a bow tie feels quite the success.
The ducks bring popcorn, a snack at the game,
While the fish in the water are never the same.

Through whispers of leaves, the laughter is loud,
As sprouting seeds jive, feeling oh-so-proud.
Their petals reveal all the quirks of their charms,
In this silly abyss, nature simply disarms.

The Flow of Yearning

A river of wishes flows over stones,
With fish that wear glasses and grumble in tones.
They dream of the sky in a splashy ballet,
While turtles wonder just when they'll play.

Near the shore, a crab tries a moonwalk at dawn,
But slips on a shell, oh what a con!
The ospreys are swooping, they've lost their cool,
Chasing trout who just think it's a lunchroom duel.

As ripples of laughter go dancing along,
The willows weave tales, a soft, swaying song.
In the breeze, a squirrel rides atop a kite,
With dreams wrapped in clouds, floating up, feeling light.

So if you hear giggles from nature's fine streams,
Just know it's the flow of our wackiest dreams.
Join in the fun, let your worries all flee,
For water's just laughing, so come take a spree!

Nature’s Canvas

On nature's broad canvas, the paint flies about,
Splashes of color that giggle and shout.
Sunsets in pinks, the sky’s wild display,
With clouds wearing hats that get blown away.

In the garden, each flower has something to say,
The tulips are gossiping, oh what a fray!
While daisies debate if they should wear shoes,
And violets gossip about their last views.

The worms in their burrows host late-night shows,
With clever remarks that nobody knows.
They bring out the laughter from deep down below,
In laughter and wiggles, the soil starts to glow.

Each drop of the rain sings a sweet little tune,
Who knew that the thunder could dance with the moon?
Nature's a painter with a comic flair,
Creating a masterpiece—joy fills the air!

The Art of Nurturing

With a sprinkle of humor, the gardener glee,
Tends to her plants, quite a sight to see.
The carrots wear shades and complain of the heat,
While peas play charades with their green little feet.

The daisies conspire with the bumblebee choir,
As tulips ask, “Who made our song backfire?”
The herbs trade their scents like they’re passing the ball,
While sunflowers wave high from their tower so tall.

The soil is a canvas where worms etch their lines,
Creating a comedy in earthy designs.
So with pruners and trowels, they all take a stand,
The garden’s a circus, oh isn’t it grand?

At dusk, as the critters head home with their rounds,
They laugh at their day in the rich, loamy grounds.
With nurturing smiles, they mix fun with the toil,
For every new sprout is a giggle in soil!

Ripples of Rejuvenation

In a garden of giggles, plants start to sway,
A bucket of laughter, they dance in the spray.
Sprouting jokes in soil, they tickle the sun,
While ants play the banjo, taking turns for fun.

A butterfly slips on a silly old hat,
Doing the cha-cha with a chatty fat cat.
The daisies are gossiping, scandals unfold,
While daisies and dandelions spin tales of old.

The sun shines a spotlight on blooms so bright,
Bouncing on raindrops, oh what a sight!
With whimsy and wonder, the roots have a ball,
In this vibrant place, laughter echoes with calls.

So raise your skinny hose, let joy overflow,
Water all the fancies that help laughter grow.
With each splash and giggle, let revelry thrive,
In the garden of dreams, where spirits arrive.

Fountains of Future

A fountain of folly bubbles and splashes,
With gnomes in a hurry, making grand crashes.
They trip over rubber ducks, quacking with glee,
While fish wear tiny sunglasses, feeling so free.

In this bubbling circus, all chaos reigns,
Tootsie rolls and marbles running like trains.
With each dribble, the future looks bright,
As giggles take flight on this water-slide night.

The frogs in tuxedos croak opera so grand,
And fireflies bring the jazz band to the stand.
Our fountains are filled with soaking-up fun,
Transforming each moment into a pun run.

So splash in the puddles, let worries all fade,
Ride on a seashell, don't be afraid!
For in these wild waters, joy's simply divine,
Where laughter's the treasure and spirits entwine.

Embracing the Elements

Oh, how the raindrops pretend they can dance,
While worms in the soil wear a muddy romance.
Each droplet a teardrop, of joy or of play,
As clouds dress in sparkles to brighten the day.

Blowing bubbles of breezes, whispering cheer,
The sun joins in play, bringing warmth ever near.
As puddles turn mirrors, reflecting the clowns,
The wind swirls like ribbons, making funny sounds.

With leaves all a-chatter, they like to conspire,
Forming a band that creates quite the choir.
In the midst of the wild, the elements cheer,
As laughter's a melody, so precious and dear.

So dance with your shadows, let giggles ignite,
In the carousel moment, feel spirits take flight.
For every raindrop is a chance for delight,
Embracing the joy that surrounds us tonight.

Essence of Eden

In the garden of humor, the flowers all smirk,
While bees steal the scene, oh what a perk!
Petals wear patterns that giggle with flair,
As grass blades gossip in the warm summer air.

The carrots play dress-up, all orange and round,
With radishes running for mayor, renowned.
They debate who can grow just a tad more absurd,
While daisies take selfies, their beauty deferred.

In this Eden of nonsense, where laughter is king,
Rainbows bloom brightly with every spring fling.
The squirrels share stories of acorns gone mad,
As laughter erupts like a joyfully fad.

So nurture the whimsy, let mirth be the seed,
In this essence of Eden where funny is freed.
So frolic through petals, let giggles unwind,
In this playful paradise, joy's never confined.

Garden of Gentle Aspirations

In the garden where daisies sway,
A gopher plays peek-a-boo all day.
The tomatoes giggle, ripe and round,
While carrots dance beneath the ground.

A ladybug wears a polka-dot hat,
And chases shadows, oh imagine that!
Bees buzz with gossip, soft and sweet,
As worms waltz on the turnip-beet.

The sunflowers gossip, heads held high,
While ants in ranks march by, oh my!
We plant our dreams beside the peas,
And hope to catch the laughter breeze.

In this patch where silliness blooms,
Even weeds whisper fun-filled tunes.
So come along and plant a smile,
In this garden, let's stay a while!

Whispered Hopes in Terra

Seeds of joy are scattered wide,
In a flower pot, a snail does slide.
With a hat made of leaves, so grand and bold,
He tells of adventures, stories untold.

The beans twist high, a climbing spree,
While frogs leap by with jubilee.
A sunflower stands with spectacles neat,
Reciting poems from its leafy seat.

A worm in stripes plays checkers slow,
While daisies compete in the garden show.
The air is filled with sweet chuckles and care,
As laughter spins threads, light as air.

Beneath a moonbeam, dreams take flight,
In crazy colors that feel just right.
So let's root for joy in every nook,
And scribble silly tales in our garden book!

Azure Drops Beneath the Sky

Bubbles burst in the great blue skies,
As raindrops giggle and do a high dive.
Puddles become stages for splashing feet,
And rubber ducks waltz, looking quite neat.

Clouds wear hats made of cotton candy,
While kites fly by, dancing all fancy.
A squirrel with an umbrella takes flight,
And giggles echo in the warm twilight.

With each drip from above, a splash of fun,
Children leap like frogs, on the run.
Joy twirls around in cackles and shouts,
As laughter blooms, there's no room for doubts.

So let the sky rain joy, bright and clear,
With every drop, let’s give a cheer.
In our puddle of dreams, let’s skip and splash,
With every giggle, let’s make a big splash!

Metallic Arc of Life

A rusty can gleams, a treasure so bright,
Spilling ideas like stars in the night.
With every tilt, a giggle unfurls,
As wishes flow like shiny pearls.

The daisies mimic the rain's goofy dance,
While blooms puff up in a luminous prance.
An eager beetle in a metallic car,
Drives through gardens, wanting to be a star!

Laughter bubbles from every hose,
As the garden twirls in a whimsical pose.
The sun beamed warmly, wearing shades,
In this circus of plants, where fun cascades.

So let's fill up our cans with giggly dreams,
And splash the world with our zany themes.
In the arc of life, shine bright, oh friend,
Through laughter and joy, our hearts will mend!

Liquid Landscapes

In gardens where the daisies play,
A bottle chases clouds away.
With giggles, plants drink up their cheer,
While worms dissolve in laughter near.

Sprinklers spin like wild ballerinas,
Chasing ducks in muddy arenas.
The sun peeks through with a wink and a grin,
As raindrops compete in a splashing spin.

The soil giggles as flowers sprout,
'Hey, look at us, we’ve grown out!'
With petals wide and colors bright,
They dance around from left to right.

But watch out for the sneaky hose,
That sprays the gardener, oh how it flows!
In this funny world of glee,
Liquid joy is free to see.

The Dance of Rain

Raindrops tap on windows like a beat,
Turning puddles into a vibrant street.
Each splash is like a tickled toe,
As raindrops giggle and water flows.

Tiny rivulets race down the glass,
Water's own version of a lively class.
The garden leans in, wanting more,
While clouds above roars and start to pour.

Frogs in hats join the muddy parade,
Jumping in sync, they're never dismayed.
With each leap, laughter fills the air,
As rainbows form with flair, oh so rare!

'Let's twirl and whirl!' cried the chuckling breeze,
While daisies elbow each other with ease.
In this hilarious watery show,
The joy of rain is all aglow.

Dark Waters, Bright Blossoms

In shadowy ponds where mushrooms sway,
Bright blossoms pop to steal the day.
With tea parties on lily pads,
The frogs wear bows and look so glad.

Glimmering fish in tuxedos swim,
While dragonflies dance on a whim.
With a tickle of breeze, the petals shake,
As flowers giggle with each tiny quake.

The trees chuckle, their branches bend,
As gnomes in the moss lend a helping hand.
Each secret sip from the water's draw,
Makes blossoms beam, 'Oh, what a flaw!'

In this laughter-filled floral spree,
Dark waters flow with such glee.
Where humor blooms in the sunlit glow,
And giggles blossom, as they grow.

Bright Blossoms

Blossoms frolic in the sunny dew,
With happy faces all fresh and new.
They swap stories with the buzzing bees,
While grass blades tickle knees with ease.

Sunflowers tall wear shades so cool,
Catching laughter, it’s their golden rule.
A sunflower whispers to a rose,
'You’re the prettiest one, everyone knows!'

In a twist of fate, a breeze doth sway,
Sending petals flying, the colorful ballet.
They flutter and flounce in bright display,
Chasing clouds with a wobbly sway.

But beware the watering hose's spray,
For petals giggle and twirl away.
In this garden, joy reigns supreme,
As flowers chatter, living the dream.

Echoes of the Garden

In a garden where laughter flows,
Echoes of whimsy in the rows.
Where tomatoes laugh and zinnias sing,
The cucumbers wear crowns, ruling their thing.

Each plant has a tale, a whimsy to share,
With whispers of dew floating in the air.
The carrots hum a joyful refrain,
While potty-mouthed daisies curse the rain.

Listen close, hear the joyous cheer,
As butterflies shout, 'We're finally here!'
With splashes of color and sounds of delight,
The garden's alive, a whimsical sight.

'Hey! I'm sprouting!' a bean shouts with glee,
While bees buzz in harmony, 'Come dance with me!'
In echoes of laughter beneath the sun's gleam,
Everyone's part of this crazy dream.

Nectar of the Night

Under the moon, a garden grows,
With giggles and snorts, the laughter flows.
Silly gnomes dance in the shadows,
Chasing fireflies in fanciful rows.

A frog croaks jokes in leafy attire,
While daisies hum tunes that never tire.
The night air twinkles with cheeky delights,
As petals twirl in their sleep so bright.

Stars wink down, sharing secrets we weave,
As flowers gossip about what they believe.
A cat named Whiskers recites with flair,
His rhymes made of dreams fill the sweet air.

Laughter in blooms, what a grand show,
A circus of colors, all in the flow.
With antics and giggles, the garden gleams,
Watered by joy, in our whimsical dreams.

Dewdrops of Desire

Tiny droplets shine like jewels of fun,
They land on leaves like a playful run.
Ants in a parade march with such pride,
While Ladybugs giggle, their laughter won't hide.

The sun peeks in, it's a warm ballet,
As flowers sway gently, ready to play.
A playful breeze tickles all the blooms,
While clouds in the distance create fanciful zooms.

Butterflies flutter with winks and grins,
Chasing their dreams on candy-striped winds.
With every splash, a muddled excuse,
For puddles of laughter, oh what a use!

In this garden of joy, mischief won't cease,
For love blooms daily, it never finds peace.
Under the sun's gaze, we dance and twirl,
With dewdrops of laughter, a magical whirl.

Blossoms of Tomorrow

In the morn, blooms wiggle with glee,
As sleepy heads stretch with a chirpy plea.
Marigolds whisper their sun-kissed hopes,
While sunflowers swaying, dream of slopes.

Worms in tuxedos compete for a role,
An earthworm pageant, that's their goal!
Petals applaud with a light-hearted cheer,
As the day unfolds with no hint of fear.

Rosy breezes tickle the soft green grass,
As daisies argue about who's the sass.
The sky dons blue, like a playful clown,
While rainbows chuckle in colors round town.

Dreams sprout in soil, each seed a delight,
With rays of the sun, they twinkle just right.
In the garden of giggles, tomorrow's embrace,
Brings blossoms of laughter, life's happy face.

Tended Visions

In a patch where giggles grow wild and free,
Plants prance around, dancing with glee.
A pickle jar full of dreams in a row,
Hopes sprout roots that want to sow.

Mice wear hats while sipping on tea,
With dainty cups made of a acorn tree.
Squirrels juggle nuts with such flair,
As butterflies gossip, their whispers declare.

Each flower's secret, a chuckle or two,
As worms share stories that sound so askew.
The sun sets slow, painting skies with delight,
As moonbeams tiptoe, ready for the night.

With visions tended, a wild jubilee,
In gardens of humor, come dance with me.
For dreams water hearts on this merry spree,
As we laugh with the blooms, so carefree.

Liquid Lullabies

In the garden, dripping bright,
A can sings in the warm sunlight.
It dances with a playful twist,
And waters flowers, none to miss.

Bumblebees hum, feeling free,
While daisies giggle, saying, "Me!"
A splash here, a sprinkle there,
Leaves a rainbow in the air.

Frogs join in with soft croaks,
Telling jokes in funny strokes.
Each droplet drops with glee and cheer,
As plants laugh loud, 'Join us here!'

When night falls, a starry show,
The can dreams big, it steals the flow.
In the moonlight, it spins around,
A watering whimsy, joy unbound.

Cultivating the Future

A garden plot with dreams anew,
Seeds buried deep, as hopes accrue.
The can takes charge, with steady pour,
Turning dirt into something more.

Sprouting beans with wicked angles,
They stretch and twist, like silly tangles.
Each plant giggles, naught to fear,
With every drop, it winks, “I’m here!”

Beetles boast with shiny shells,
Trading jokes, oh, how it swells!
The can, a mastermind of schemes,
Turns squishy soil into wild dreams.

Little sprouts, the future’s pride,
Laugh together, side by side.
With every splash, that can will find,
A world where laughter’s interlined.

Harmony in the Garden

Under sun, the garden sways,
The can hums in joyful ways.
Cabbages in silly hats,
Joking softly with the sprats.

Flowers sway, their colors bright,
Planning parties every night.
With every splash that hits the ground,
A tickle wriggles all around.

Pests in boots do line dance moves,
While soil whispers in sweet grooves.
The can, a maestro of the green,
Conducts a show, a sight unseen.

Nature swirls in merry tune,
Beneath the watchful eye of moon.
In the garden, laughter rings,
As every plant with joy now sings.

The Magic in Moisture

A can full of tricks and laughs,
Sprays water as it takes its baths.
With every pour, it sprinkles glee,
Making snails smile, fancy-free.

On rainy days, oh what a sight,
The weeds wear hats, all day and night.
Dancing droplets, so surreal,
Turning chores into a meal.

The carrots tell the jokes they know,
While turnips giggle, “Go, go, go!”
Caught in a water ballet's sway,
Every plant shines bright today.

In the end, with hearts so wide,
The garden's magic cannot hide.
With laughter bubbling, dreams are spun,
As hydration makes the world more fun.

Serenade of the Soil's Heartbeat

In the garden, the soil starts to sway,
Worms audition for a Broadway play.
Each droplet that falls, a comical tune,
Plants munch popcorn under the moon.

Roses wear hats, daisies dance in their shoes,
The carrots debate if they'll ever lose.
Each sunflower giggles at a beet's big round,
As puddles do polka on soft, marshy ground.

Ants don tiny shades, strut like they own,
While raindrops call out, 'Come join our grown!'
Every thimble of soil whispers a jest,
As worms weave their tales, we're surely blessed.

So laugh with the leaves, let your humor bloom,
In this garden of giggles, make room for the zoom.
For in every good sprout, there's joy to be found,
In the soil's warm embrace, all hearts dance around.

The Pulse Beneath the Surface

Beneath the mulch, a party thrives,
Earthworms groove, while the beetle jives.
Bubbles rise up, like laughter in bloom,
They're plotting a heist on that pesky broom!

Beneath the roots, a festival spins,
As raindrops clap for the tiny wins.
Mushrooms joke about their odd-shaped hats,
While snails take bets on which way the cat sat.

Puddles reflect a cosmic ballet,
Splashing good humor, come join the fray!
Ants in a conga line, oh what a sight,
Under the moon, they dance through the night.

So dip your toes in this mirthful stew,
Where life loves laughter, and laughs love you.
Beneath the surface, there's joy to be shared,
In every whimsy, feel the pulse unbarred.

Garden of Whispers

In the corner plot, whispers galore,
The lettuce relates how it learnt to roar.
Tomatoes giggle in shades of red,
While peas throw parties in their green bed.

Cucumbers tease with a cool, crisp sigh,
Zucchini plays hide and seek, oh my!
Basil tells secrets while the thyme rolls its eyes,
Where herbs spin tales beneath sunny skies.

Every morning dew, a soft chuckle's spark,
As radishes plan a late-night lark.
Lettuce wraps gossip in a leafy embrace,
While pumpkins exchange jokes, full of grace.

So stroll through the rows where the blooms love to chat,
In this garden of whispers, enjoy a laugh or pat.
For in nature's bench, humor's always in style,
And the crops are in stitches, all the while.

Liquid Ambitions

A jug of dreams spills over the ledge,
As flowers embark on a wacky pledge.
Each splash a giggle, a goofy parade,
While daisies take selfies in sun's golden shade.

Drips from a cloud, oh what a delight,
As ferns do cha-chas in morning light.
The pond reflects secrets, with fish as the crew,
Planning a caper on swan's sauce à deux.

Streams hum a tune, oh so absurd,
While frogs form a band, each note just a word.
With splashes and splatters, they frolic and cheer,
Watering can hums like it's got no fear.

So raise a glass to this liquid spree,
Where every droplet dreams wild and free.
In the dance of the raindrops, find muse and laughter,
For in liquid ambitions, joy comes after.

Dreams in the Dew

In the garden, where weeds play,
I left my thoughts to drift away.
Twirling daisies, under the sun,
Chasing bees, now that’s pure fun!

Juggling droplets, like a game,
Each one whispers, 'We are the same.'
Hopping puddles, shoes that squeak,
Giggles echo, soft and weak.

Shrubs are laughing, worms do sigh,
“Grow taller!” they shout, reaching for the sky.
With all the sprigs and tiny leaves,
I plan my world, or so it seems!

So bring your trowel, let’s make a mess,
In the garden, life’s a jest.
Each little sprout, a tale to tell,
Of dreams unfurling, oh so well!

Tendrils of Tomorrow

A sprout peeked out with a little grin,
Said, "I can’t wait for my game to begin!"
Twisting and curling, oh what a sight,
Reaching for stars, while dodging the light.

The grass, it chuckles, tickling toes,
“Hey there, buddy, don’t trip on your woes!”
I’ll water the dreams with laughter and cheer,
Who knew sprouts could be so sincere?

Planting a vision, took off my shoe,
Can’t let the soil get lonely too!
Magical whispers swirl with the breeze,
Hopes bloom brightly, just like the trees.

So dance, little roots, in your soil so deep,
While I giggle at thoughts, in my mind, they leap.
Dreams like seedlings, frolicking free,
Let's water the future, just you and me!

Essence of the Rain

Pitter-patter, oh what a sound,
Raindrops giggle, falling down bound.
In rubber boots, I splash and spin,
Making muddy swirls, let the fun begin!

Clouds hold secrets, what do they hide?
Rainbows tangle, in bright colors, they glide.
Chasing droplets, trying to catch,
Every splash sends me back to scratch.

The puddles mirror, each crazy face,
Wondering where is my happy place?
Each raindrop serves a crazy dance,
Inviting all to join its prance.

Splashes swirling, oh what delight,
Essence of joy flows, day and night.
Water and laughter, what a pair,
In this silly world, free as air!

The Elixir of Growth

With a sprinkle and twist, I set out to roam,
Through flower beds, I feel right at home.
Shovels and laughter, what a sweet brew,
Digging for dreams, hope springs anew.

The sun is a friend, grinning so bright,
It tickles the leaves, spreading pure light.
Seedlings are singing, wearing their best,
Trying to bloom in this lively jest.

Comically green, the veggies parade,
Potatoes in sunglasses, all dressed for trade.
Goal of the garden? A fun, sweet spree!
To taste all the magic that's growing in me!

So pour out your laughter, splatter a grin,
With every small flower, let joy begin.
The elixir of growth, it's silly and grand,
It’s the best kind of garden, just as we planned!

Petals of Promise

A jug in hand, I sway with glee,
My garden waits, it's thirsty, you see.
With every pour, a splash of cheer,
I dance around, not a worry nor fear.

The daisies giggle, the roses tease,
As puddles form, I drop to my knees.
What fun it is, a silly spree,
My flowers laugh, they bloom just for me.

Oh look! A daffodil wears a hat,
It's soaked in style, and how about that?
I shake my can, rain falls from above,
My plants all shimmy, oh how they move!

Tomorrow's sun brings more delight,
A rainbow sparkles, oh what a sight!
With petals bright and dreams so wide,
I water joy, my garden's pride.

Curated Currents

In the yard, I reign supreme,
Pouring water, living the dream.
Catch the drips, as I leap about,
My watering can – a splashy clout!

The tulips cheer, the lilacs clap,
Each drop a joke, a funny mishap.
I float my way, like a fish on land,
With every sprinkle, I have a plan.

A garden party, everyone joins,
With miniature slides and playful coins.
Squirting friends, it's pure delight,
In a droplet dance, we splash all night!

Each petal doused in laughter's glow,
Nature's smiles, the best kind of show.
So I douse away, and in between,
A funny bond, with all that's green!

Harvesting Hopes

With my can, I talk to greens,
They whisper back, with giggly scenes.
I sprinkle dreams on every row,
Waiting for magic, put on the show!

My lettuce drips, a comical sight,
Winking at veggies, oh what a night.
Mischief sprouts, the carrots conspire,
In this whimsical plot, dreams never tire.

The zucchini wears a polka dot dress,
While cucumbers murmur in soft caress.
They dance in the breeze, like tiny fools,
Harvesting dreams from laughter-filled pools.

Oh, the joy of a garden so bright,
In the sunlight, we take flight.
With drops of hope, we fill the ground,
In this playful garden, magic is found!

Nature's Tender Touch

I tip my can, with clumsy grace,
A splash of joy in this happy place.
Flowers giggle, as they bloom so wide,
Nature's touch, I tour the guide.

Each droplet tells a secret tale,
Of raindrops once that danced like a whale.
My daisies prance, their petals flurry,
In this garden, there's never a hurry.

With twists and turns, I make my way,
I trip on roots, a funny display.
The sunbeam shines, in golden hue,
My garden blooms, with laughter anew.

So here’s to watering with glee,
Fun in nature, just you and me.
Each plant a friend, we laugh and sing,
In this silly world, joy's the king!

Silver Streams

In gardens dense, a curious sight,
A metal pot, oh what a fright!
It spills and spills with glee, what fun,
Do plants now dance, or is it just one?

The daisies giggle, the roses hum,
As droplets dance, they start to strum.
"More water, more joy!" the petals cheer,
While worms in the soil whisper, "Oh dear!"

A dragonfly dips, a squirrel prances,
While hummingbirds waltz, in floral trances.
A spill here, a splash there, pure delight,
Little green beans plan their flight!

And as the sun begins to fade,
The metal pot starts to parade.
For in this garden of laughter and cheer,
Who knew a can could hold such beer?

Radiant Roots

Beneath the soil, secrets reside,
With roots that wriggle, they laugh and slide.
“Water us now!” the carrots implore,
But the daisies just giggle, “We want more!”

“Oh dear!” said the lettuce, “Did you hear?
The garden’s holding a party, oh dear!
With splashes of sunshine and drops of glee,
I hope they serve salads, just for me!”

A sprinkle here, a puddle there,
The radishes rumble with wild flair.
“Just a tad more!” the veggies scream,
As they sway along in a muddy dream.

With every pour, the fun expands,
It’s a riot of roots with playful hands.
So let’s raise a cup, and even a sprout,
For gardening's a laugh, without a doubt!

Echoes of Earth

In a garden filled with life, oh my!
A sprout may sing, and a carrot might cry.
With water drizzled, they sway and shake,
"A little dip, for goodness' sake!"

The tulips tease the daffodils,
"Look at us dance, and feel those thrills!"
While gentle rains come down to play,
The soil whispers secrets in the fray.

"Oh, what's that?" the radish snorted,
"Is it the water? I feel shorted!"
They giggled and squirmed in muddy beds,
While beetroot blushed, parading in reds.

So, as you sprinkle in this turf,
Remember the joys beneath the surf.
With every drop, a story spins,
Where laughter blooms, and joy begins!

Waves of Wonder

A garden wave, oh how it flows!
With plants that giggle in a row.
"Let's surf on sprinkles!" the beans all shout,
While lettuce leaves get tossed about.

The water sways, it bubbles and rolls,
While marigolds dance, and parsley strolls.
"More waves! More fun!" the daisies hoot,
As the tomatoes laugh in their juicy suits.

The sun explorer drips from high,
"Catch me if you can!", it starts to fly.
And in the squishy, mucky delight,
Even the weeds hold hands, so tight!

So, raise your cans to bubbles and pops,
In our garden kingdom, the laughter never stops.
With waves of wonder, and spritzing cheer,
We'll water our dreams, year after year!

Pouring Passion into Parched Soil

With my can set upon a shelf,
I watered all but my own self.
The daisies laughed, the roses sighed,
While I just wondered, 'Where’s my ride?'

The neighbors yelled, 'What’s that sound?'
As I sang to weeds, tumbling around.
A sprinkler danced, I lost my grace,
Spilling dreams all over the place.

I held the spout and made a wish,
'Grow me a garden, you little fish!'
But all I got were knots and tangles,
And chattering gnomes with wild eyed wrangles.

So here I stand, a chuckle afloat,
With droplets glimmering, I take note.
Master of mess, receiver of laughs,
In my dreamland, I still water staffs.

Essence of Tomorrow’s Blossoms

I dream of golden blooms so bright,
Yet drip my can all through the night.
The snails parade, I’m on their route,
As I blunder about, legs in a drought.

Each splash's a giggle, a bubbling thrill,
But oh, those daisies, they always chill.
Too much attention, they start to pout,
While tomatoes throw a late-night bout.

Pansies cheer as I slip and slide,
In this flower race, I’m the clown they bide.
Each blossom’s secret fuels the spree,
For tomorrow’s essence is laughter, you see.

So pour I shall, with jest and cheer,
With every drop, I conquer my fear.
In the garden’s embrace, my spirit romps,
My dreams in blooms, with funny little stomps.

Dappled Light on Ambitions

A sprinkle of dreams in morning light,
I aimed for heights, oh what a sight!
But my ambitions, like weeds, they grew,
Instead of flowers, I flowered up stew.

The sunlight flickers, bugle sounds yell,
I dance among sprouts, oh can't do well!
Slipping on dirt, embracing the mire,
With every green leaf, I plot my empire.

The clouds above are my joke-telling kin,
As they rain down quips, let the chaos begin!
Ambitions waver, but not my grin,
Watch as I tumble and leap from within.

With dappled light casting shadows anew,
My garden's a circus; it's charmingly true.
I gather my dreams with humor and glee,
For each goofy sip from my can is free.

Reservoir of the Heart's Whispers

In the reservoir of giggles, I dwell,
Pouring secrets and stories to tell.
A splash of laughter, a spritz of joy,
As I garden like some clumsy toy.

With whispers of petals, I dance in the breeze,
Confetti of blooms that never cease.
But watch your step, don't trip on a sprout,
Laughter erupts with every route out.

The whispers grow louder, what's that I hear?
A chorus of petals, my heart's warm cheer.
With buckets of giggles and can full of dreams,
I splash joy like sunlight, or so it seems.

So join in the frolic, the mirth, the fun,
Where whimsy and nature merge into one.
In the reservoir wide, my heart does throng,
With each secret whispered, I burst into song.

Unfurling the Sunlit Siphon

In a garden where giggles bloom,
A little jug with a colorful plume.
It tiptoes around with glee so bright,
Sprinkling laughter and delight.

It squirts at the daisies, they dance in joy,
Chasing the drops like a playful toy.
The petunias chuckle, the roses hum tunes,
As sunshine sprinkles like sweet balloons.

Oh, what a sight, this whimsical spree,
With a spout that grins as wide as can be.
Each drip is a giggle, each splash is a cheer,
Creating a symphony garden-gathered here.

Essence Quenching Earth's Thirst

In a world where droplets hold their breath,
A quirky jug, defying death.
It sways and swerves with utmost flair,
Sipping the soil, without a care.

"Chug, chug," it sings, "I've got a dream!"
"To sprinkle the flowers with a bubbly beam."
As blades of grass snicker and sway,
It glides along, come what may.

A dance that swishes, a twirl in the sun,
With muddy splashes, what fun has begun?
The earth drinks deeply, oh what a sight,
As giggles echo from morning to night.

Dew-Kissed Paths to Potential

Rolling along with a capricious pout,
A silly jug, with no doubt.
It skips over stones, bypasses the weeds,
Watering dreams like wildflower seeds.

Chortles erupt as it spills and spills,
Covering gardens with giggly thrills.
Each droplet bursts with dreams so absurd,
Like ticklish waves of a playful bird.

“Soon you’ll grow big, just wait and see!”
It laughs, pouring joy with wild jubilee.
Tiny sprouts grinning, reaching for fun,
Thanks to the antics of the jester run.

The Cycle of Fluid Fantasies

In a whirl of sunlight, it takes a spin,
A jolly jug with a mischievous grin.
Patting the plants, "You'll be a surprise!"
As splashes create little giddy highs.

Sippity-splash, what a silly sight,
Chasing the ants in pure delight.
"Oops, not the hose, my mistake indeed!"
Said the jug, as it giggled, sowing the seed.

It twirls and dances on dew-kissed grass,
Rolling in puddles, letting time pass.
Each drip, a chuckle, each sprout, a cheer,
In this merry world, dreams grow sincere.

Petals in the Rain

When raindrops fall like tiny clowns,
They dance upon the green, not frowns.
A flower hat, quite out of place,
Winks at the sky with a splash of grace.

The daisies giggle, the roses sway,
In this silly shower, they want to play.
A bumblebee dons a raincoat bright,
Buzzing around in pure delight.

The puddles laugh, they're full of cheer,
Reflecting faces; is that you, dear?
The world is drenched, but spirits soar,
With every splash, we adore the lure.

So let it rain, who cares if we're wet?
A bloom's delight, no need to fret.
In petals' dance, we find our glee,
Laughter sprouting, wild and free.

Flowing Dreams

In a stream of giggles, the frogs do cheer,
As raindrops tickle their webbed frontiers.
A fish in a tuxedo swims with flair,
Cracking a smile in water's fair.

The willows wave like they're saying, "Hi!"
A snail in a bowtie flashes by.
With dreams afloat on every bubble,
Nature's humor finds no trouble.

The clouds pass by, with silly grins,
Pouring giggles on all their kin.
While worms in the mud do a twisty dance,
In this bright puddle of pure romance.

Under the sun, raindrops glisten,
Flowers and bugs form a choir, they listen.
With laughter echoing far and wide,
Flowing dreams take us for a ride.

Nature's Canvas of Color

A painter with splashes, a palette of wet,
The brush of the rain makes a vibrant offset.
A sunflower giggles in hues of delight,
Tickled by raindrops that glimmer at night.

The violets chuckle, they wiggle and sway,
While dandelions hop like kids at play.
In a world where colors all come to tease,
Mother Nature's art brings us to our knees.

Crayons of water draw lines on the ground,
With each droplet splattering, joy's all around.
Butterflies flutter, a rainbow parade,
Painting the sky where dreams never fade.

Through laughter and color, we're stuck in the groove,
Nature's canvas with every move.
So let's splash along with a joyful scream,
In this brilliant art, we live our dream.

Lush Drizzles

When it's drizzling, we jump with glee,
What a splash party, come join with me!
A gopher in galoshes takes a grand leap,
While a daffodil giggles and tickles her sleep.

The clouds throw confetti; it's a stormy fête,
With ducks in the puddles who never hesitate.
A squirrel in a slicker does pirouettes,
All in good fun, no regrets.

Watch out for puddles, they're sneaky and wide,
One wrong step and you're on a wet ride!
But laughter's infectious, just look at the trees,
They sway and they giggle; oh, what a breeze.

The world is a playground when the skies are gray,
With raindrops as friends, forever we play.
In lush drizzles, we find our cheer,
A wet and wild world, oh, let's persevere!

Lifeblood of Flora

In the garden, sprouting glee,
With a sprinkle here, a splash there,
The daisies giggle, saying, "Whee!"
While the roses twirl without a care.

Oh, the bees buzz like tiny clowns,
As they sip on nectar's sweet tease,
They wear little floral crowns,
Dancing 'round, just like the leaves.

A hose becomes a playful snake,
Twisting 'round the pots to play,
While children laugh and the flowers shake,
As they drink and bloom through the day.

Each drop a joke that nature tells,
As the colors burst in sunlit streams,
With soil and laughter, all is well,
In this funny world of leafy dreams.

The Gentle Embrace

Underneath a wide blue sky,
A can makes circles, oh so grand,
With every pour, the flowers sigh,
As love falls gently from the hand.

The tulips hoot, the lilies laugh,
While the daisies take a little dip,
In puddled joy, they share a path,
Like kids all riding on a ship.

Every swing, a joyous dance,
The droplets twinkle like an ode,
Flowers prance in a silly trance,
As they drink from the joyful load.

When I water, they burst with cheer,
Saying, "Thank you, we're feeling bright!"
With chatty petals year after year,
We bloom and giggle in daylight.

Fluid Visions

In the garden's wild delight,
A can with dreams begins to flow,
Bubbling laughter, flowers ignite,
With every sprinkle, colors grow.

A cloud of giggles drips from leaves,
As daisies quip and violets tease,
They splash and twirl, it's all a breeze,
While nature hums in joyful keys.

Rain dances down in a jolly spree,
Only to meet a cat's surprise,
As muddy paws make a sight to see,
Painting joy with sunlit skies.

Oh, to water is pure, sweet fun,
With jokes in blossoms, roots so spry,
In this world where laughter's spun,
The plants tap dance to every sigh.

Chasing the Light

In search of sun, the flowers leak,
With every drip, a joke unfolds,
Dancing petals, ever so chic,
As the can sings, the garden molds.

The carrots wiggle, the herbs poke fun,
While weeds whisper, "We wish to stay!"
A little sprinkle under the sun,
Makes them prance, it’s blooming play.

With flicks and flutters, it’s quite a scene,
The lettuce snickers, the beans make plans,
For a yearly festival of green,
In the company of merry fans.

Each drop of joy, a spark of glee,
As I water with a mischievous grin,
In this garden, we all agree,
Nature's laughter is where we begin.

Delicate Streams of Possibility

A can with a spout, oh what a sight,
Pouring out dreams, both day and night.
It spills out ideas, like puddles of cheer,
And splits the sun's shine, like laughter we hear.

A tip here, a tilt there, it's all in the flow,
Watering hopes that we dare to sow.
With every splash, a giggle takes flight,
As petals dance wild, in pure delight.

Its rusty old handle, a story it brings,
Of flowers and whispers, and peculiar things.
A carrot once dreamed of becoming a fry,
While daisies plot world tours under the sky.

So fill it with joy, let the fun overflow,
This can full of dreams, with a mischievous glow.
As nature laughs on, with a wink and a beam,
We'll water the seedlings of each silly dream.

The Fertile Vessel's Song

Oh vessel of laughter, with a jolly old cap,
You sprinkle my garden, such a comical map!
With each little sip from your funky old spout,
You water all giggles, there’s never a doubt.

Each droplet a chorus, for worms in the ground,
They wiggle and jiggle, oh what a sound!
Tending to the daisies, you truly do rock,
They sway in their blooms, like a jolly old flock.

A dance with the daisies, a waltz with the ferns,
While weeds hold their breath, and politely take turns.
Your cartwheeling rain, such a whimsical thing,
Turns soil into stories, where laughter will sing.

So let’s fill you up, with a rainbow or two,
Your laughter, dear vessel, brings life anew.
In gardens of giggles, we’ll splash and we’ll play,
For happiness blooms on a sunny old day.

Drizzle of Envisioned Futures

A flick of the wrist, and here comes the fun,
Rainbows and giggles, from the shining sun.
I dream of a garden, where silly things grow,
With squawking blue crows, yelling out "hello!"

The spout is a rocket, taking seeds for a ride,
Each drop is a thought, where wild wishes reside.
Potatoes in tutus, what a whimsical sight,
As carrots bounce by, under soft morning light.

A sprinkle of hopes in a can of delight,
Makes for the best blooms on a starry night.
Oh, the laughter it brings, oh the joys that it yields,
As each silly vegetable thwarts the harsh fields.

So gather your dreams in this playful old can,
Keep watering wishes, as only you can.
With love and with laughter, we'll plant every seed,
And watch as they blossom, from each quirky deed.

Canopy of Liquid Wishes

Under the trees, with a jovial splash,
A dance of the drops, oh what a bash!
Leaves giggle softly, in whispers they scheme,
While we water their wishes, like a sparkling dream.

The clouds are our friends, they send down the cheer,
Sprinkling round joy for the blooms to appear.
A can full of chuckles, with a twist and a turn,
Sprouts tickle our toes, while the daisies all yearn.

Each dribble a chance, for silly things to thrive,
A garden of giggles, where imaginations strive.
Oh flowers, oh bugs, come share in the fun,
With laughter and dreams, we'll brighten the sun.

Let's gather our wishes, let the watering begin,
With a splash of stardust, a sprinkle of grin.
For joy in the garden is all that we need,
As we dance with the droplets, planting whimsical seed.

Raindrops and Reveries

A leaky pot with a fanciful grin,
Plays tricks on plants, let the fun begin.
Puppies chase puddles, splashing with glee,
As daisies giggle and join the spree.

Moonlit showers bring a splashy dance,
As crickets croon in an aerial prance.
Squirrels dive in for a quick water cheer,
While frogs in tuxedos clap without fear.

The cat tries to sip with a silly wide face,
But ends up in chaos—what a wet race!
A beetle slips in for a boisterous glide,
While the ants host a poolside giggling ride.

The sun comes out, oh, what a sight,
As rainbows peek in, cloudy delight.
With dreams of the day now floating on air,
Our gardening circus has giggles to share.

Soothing Sprinklers

Sprinklers whirl in a frolicking show,
Dancing in gardens, they put on a flow.
Gnomes with their hats get a sudden spray,
While daisies bounce up, ready to play.

A hose full of dreams pours forth with glee,
Tickling the toes of a hapless bee.
Children run wild as the water takes flight,
Turning mundane into pools of delight.

Piglets in mud want a sloshy embrace,
While butterflies flutter, making a race.
The sun shines bright, but let’s not forget,
The chaos today might end up a wet bet.

Giggling echoes ring out in the air,
As tomato plants wiggle, the world’s their chair.
With every drop, laughter spreads like cheer,
In this tale of spray, the fun is clear!

Enchanted Earth

In a garden so wild, a strange sight unfolds,
Flowers have secrets, or so I'm told.
A tulip does cartwheels, a rose takes a leap,
While tomatoes are singing, oh what a heap!

Earthworms are dancing, they twist and they twirl,
With fidgety roots that spin and swirl.
The daisies in dresses laugh under the sun,
As a carrot stands tall, bragging it's fun.

The well was a pint-sized comedy club,
With jokes full of puns, it's the watering hub.
The star of the night? A squash on a quest,
Delivering laughter from east to the west.

As colors collide, it's a riotous sight,
In this land of blossoms, everything's bright.
So if you feel sluggish, come take a peek,
At this playful paradise where plants love to speak.

Untamed Hydration

A monster of hoses goes wiggle and squirt,
Creating a splash that ends up in dirt.
Turtles take slides down mounds with delight,
As raindrops keep laughing, a hilarious sight.

Hydration runs wild—oh, what a thrill,
With puddles that shimmer, let’s chase on the hill.
Hopping like rabbits, we leap with a cheer,
While marigolds wink, the party's right here!

A leaf on a mission to catch every drop,
Accidentally opening the rain dance shop.
With dancing dandelions, oh what a spree,
The flow is contagious, it sparkles with glee.

In chaotic rhythms, the garden erupts,
While dew-decked critters perform as they strut.
So grab your own jug, let the fun unfold,
In this land of hydration, where laughter is gold.

Sowing the Clouds

I planted a cloud in my backyard,
It sprouted jokes, all fluffy and hard.
The raindrops danced, so silly and bright,
Splashing my garden with pure delight.

I sneezed at a storm, it rumbled and laughed,
Poured out a giggle, a joyfully daft.
My flowers wiggled in fits of glee,
As butterflies joined for a comedy spree.

Sunshine looked down, a smirk on its face,
Said, ‘Keep up the antics, it’s quite the race!’
A daffodil chimed, 'Let’s throw in some fun,'
As the clouds up above began to run.

With dreams of the sky, I prance and I sway,
In my giggling garden, I frolic and play.
Each seed a laugh, each bloom a cheer,
In this zany patch, there’s nothing to fear!

A Symphony of Sprouts

In a pot, I heard a tiny hum,
A symphony started, here they come!
Tiny sprouts dancing, in chorus they sing,
Popping up rhythms, it's a lively spring.

The carrots are crooning, the peas do some taps,
While radishes march in their tiny wee caps.
Lettuce is laughing, doing the twist,
In this green concert, it's hard to resist.

With every sprinkle, oh what a sound,
Melodies sprout from the rich, fertile ground.
Tomatoes on bass, cucumbers play lead,
Together they make quite the quirky breed.

In this playful farm, where laughter is grown,
Each note a delight, every tune overblown.
Pulling weeds feels like a dance of delight,
In my garden symphony, everything's right!

Beneath the Canopy

Beneath the big leaves, the giggles arise,
Where squirrels tell secrets and whisper their lies.
The mushrooms are facets of hats for the toads,
Each critter and plant just lightens the load.

A dragonfly buzzes, off-key with a spin,
While ants form a band, making music within.
The sunbeams are clapping, the shadows take part,
In this shady nook, there's a festival heart.

A rabbit hops in with a twirl and a scoot,
Claiming the stage in its fluffy, sly suit.
The grass tickles toes, the crickets compose,
A raucous performance where everyone knows.

In the garden's embrace, we all lose our cares,
With laughter resounding, no room for despairs.
Under the canopy, joy drifts like streams,
We dance with the breeze and live out our dreams!

Cascade of Wishes

I tossed a coin in the puddle so round,
Wishing for giggles to flood all around.
The ripples burst forth with a swish and a splash,
Carrying chuckles like a light-hearted dash.

A duck quacked a tune, it played with great flair,
While frogs did a jig, splashing water everywhere.
The twinkle of wishes flowed free on the breeze,
As laughter cascaded like drops from the trees.

I wished for a rainbow that giggles at night,
To blanket the town in a spectrum of light.
And every kind wish was a splash in the dark,
With dreams tumbling down like a fairytale lark.

In a puddle world where we relish and roam,
Each splash brings us closer to laughter and home.
With wishes like water, this joy paints our scene,
Creating a cascade where nothing's routine!

www.ingramcontent.com/pod-product-compliance
Lightning Source LLC
Chambersburg PA
CBHW070305120526
44590CB00017B/2571
* 9 7 8 1 8 0 5 8 1 3 4 3 9 *